Chairman Murphy, Ranking Member DeGette, and Members of the Subcommittee:

I am pleased to be here today to discuss our work examining fraud in the Medicare program.[1] We have designated Medicare as a high-risk program since 1990, in part because we found the program's size and complexity make it vulnerable to fraud, waste, and abuse.[2] Although there have been convictions for multimillion-dollar schemes that defrauded the Medicare program, the extent of the problem is unknown.[3] There are no reliable estimates of the extent of fraud in the Medicare program or for the health care industry as a whole. By its very nature, fraud is difficult to detect, as those involved are engaged in intentional deception. For example, a provider submitting a fraudulent claim may include false documentation to substantiate a service not provided, and thus the claim may appear valid on its face. Fraud may also involve payments made to beneficiaries to obtain their Medicare number for fraudulent billing purposes. Although the full extent of the problem is unknown, it is clear that, as one of the largest programs in the federal government, the Medicare program is vulnerable to fraud, contributing to its fiscal problems.

In 2013, Medicare financed health care services for approximately 51 million individuals at a cost of about $604 billion and reported some of the largest estimates of improper payments among federal programs—payments that either were made in an incorrect amount or should not

---

[1]Medicare is the federally financed health insurance program for persons age 65 or over, certain individuals with disabilities, and individuals with end-stage renal disease.

[2]In 1990, we began to report on government operations that we identified as "high risk" for serious weaknesses in areas that involve substantial resources and provide critical services to the public. Medicare has been included among such programs since 1990. See GAO, *High-Risk Series: An Update*, GAO-13-283 (Washington, D.C.: February 2013).

[3]Fraud involves an intentional act or representation to deceive with the knowledge that the action or representation could result in gain.

GAO-14-712T

have been made at all.[4] The Centers for Medicare & Medicaid Services (CMS), the agency within the Department of Health and Human Services (HHS) that oversees Medicare, has estimated that improper payments in the Medicare program were almost $50 billion in fiscal year 2013, about $5 billion higher than in 2012.[5] Improper payments may be a result of fraud, waste, or abuse, but it is important to distinguish that the $50 billion in estimated improper payments reported by CMS in fiscal year 2013 is not an estimate of fraud in Medicare.[6] Reported improper payment estimates include many types of payments that should not have been made or were made in an incorrect amount such as overpayments, underpayments, and payments that were not adequately documented.

Since its inception, Medicare has been administered largely by contractors with federal oversight, and these contractors have a responsibility to help ensure Medicare program integrity.[7] CMS must oversee their efforts to help ensure proper payments and address the program's many vulnerabilities, which include service- or system-specific weaknesses that can lead to payment errors, including those due to

---

[4]Improper payments may be a result of fraud, waste, or abuse. They are any payments that should not have been made or that were made in an incorrect amount (including overpayments and underpayments) under statutory, contractual, administrative, or other legally applicable requirements. This definition includes any payment to an ineligible recipient, any payment for an ineligible good or service, any duplicate payment, any payment for a good or service not received (except where authorized by law), and any payment that does not account for credit for applicable discounts. Improper Payments Elimination and Recovery Act of 2010, Pub. L. No. 111-204, § 2(e), 124 Stat. 2224, 2227 (codified at 31 U.S.C. § 3321 note).

[5]A list of abbreviations used in this statement is provided in app. I.

[6]Waste includes inaccurate payments for services, such as unintentional duplicate payments. Abuse represents actions inconsistent with acceptable business or medical practices.

[7]The Medicare program consists of four parts: A, B, C, and D. Medicare Parts A and B are known as Medicare fee-for-service (FFS). Medicare Part A covers hospital and other inpatient stays. Medicare Part B is optional, and covers hospital outpatient, physician, and other services. Medicare beneficiaries have the option of obtaining coverage for Medicare services from private health plans that participate in Medicare Advantage—Medicare's managed care program—also known as Part C. All Medicare beneficiaries may purchase coverage for outpatient prescription drugs under Part D, either as a stand-alone benefit or as part of a Medicare Advantage plan. Contractors are responsible for administering Medicare FFS claims and conducting activities to reduce improper payments.

fraud.[8] If CMS suspects that providers or suppliers are billing fraudulently, it can take action through its contractors, including suspending claims payment, revoking billing privileges, or referring cases to law enforcement for investigation.[9]

My statement today focuses on the progress made and important steps to be taken by CMS to reduce fraud in Medicare. It is primarily based on our Medicare program integrity products issued and recommendations made from April 2004 through May 2014,[10] as well as selected updates on actions CMS has taken, and will focus on progress related to three key strategies we have identified as important to reducing fraud, waste, and abuse, and ultimately improper payments:[11]

- strengthening provider and supplier enrollment standards and procedures,

- improving prepayment and postpayment review of claims, and

- addressing identified vulnerabilities.

In June 2014, we updated information based on new regulations regarding enrollment of certain providers in Medicare by examining public documents. Our work for this statement and the products on which it was based was conducted in accordance with generally accepted government auditing standards. Those standards require that we plan and perform the

---

[8]CMS defines vulnerabilities to the Medicare program as issues that can lead to fraud, waste, or abuse, which can be either specific, such as providers receiving multiple payments as a result of incorrect coding for a service, or general and programwide, such as weaknesses in online application processes. An example of a vulnerability that leads to improper payments is providers billing for more than one blood transfusion in a hospital outpatient setting for a Medicare beneficiary in a day, which Medicare policy does not allow.

[9]In this testimony, the term *provider* includes entities such as hospitals or physicians, and *supplier* means entities such as ambulance service providers, mammography centers, and entities that supply Medicare beneficiaries with durable medical equipment, prosthetics, orthotics, and supplies (DMEPOS), such as walkers and wheelchairs. This testimony will use the term providers and suppliers when referring to all Medicare providers and suppliers but will specify other suppliers, such as DMEPOS suppliers, when necessary.

[10]The products listed at the end of this statement contain detailed information on the various methodologies used in our work.

[11]See GAO, *Program Integrity: Further Action Needed to Address Vulnerabilities in Medicaid and Medicare Programs*, GAO-12-803T (Washington, D.C.: June 7, 2012).

audit to obtain sufficient, appropriate evidence to provide a reasonable basis for our findings and conclusions based on our audit objectives. We believe that the evidence obtained provides a reasonable basis for our findings and conclusions based on our audit objectives.

Background

Since 1996, Congress has taken important steps to increase Medicare program integrity funding and oversight, including the establishment of the Medicare Integrity Program. Table 1 summarizes several key congressional actions.

Table 1: Key Congressional Actions to Increase Medicare Program Integrity Funding and Oversight

Year	Congressional action	Statute
1996	Created the Medicare Integrity Program and established dedicated funding for activities to address fraud, waste, and abuse in federal health care programs, including Medicare[a]	Health Insurance Portability and Accountability Act of 1996[b]
2003	Directed CMS to conduct a 3-year demonstration project on the use of recovery audit contractors (RAC) for identifying and recouping Medicare underpayments and overpayments	Medicare Prescription Drug, Improvement, and Modernization Act of 2003[c]
2006	Required CMS to implement a national RAC program by January 1, 2010	Tax Relief and Health Care Act of 2006[d]
2010	Provided additional funding for program integrity activities and, among other things • established new provider enrollment requirements • required CMS to extend the Medicare RACs to Parts C and D of the Medicare program • required CMS to develop core elements for provider compliance programs • authorized surety bond requirements for certain Medicare providers[e]	Patient Protection and Affordable Care Act (PPACA)[f]
2010	Required Medicare fee-for-service to begin using predictive analytics to identify and prevent fraud[g]	Small Business Jobs Act of 2010[h]

Source: GAO analysis of selected federal laws. | GAO-14-712T

[a]The fund is known as the Health Care Fraud and Abuse Control account.

[b]Pub. L. No. 104-191, §§ 201(b)-202, 110 Stat. 1936, 1993-98 (codified at 42 U.S. C. §§ 1395i(k), 1395ddd).

[c]Pub. L. No. 108-173, § 306, 117 Stat. 2066, 2256-57.

[d]Pub. L. No. 109-432, div B., title III, § 302, 120 Stat. 2922, 2991-92 (codified at 42 U.S.C. § 1395 ddd(h)).

[e]A surety bond is a three-party agreement in which a company, known as a surety, agrees to compensate the bondholder if the bond purchaser fails to keep a specified promise.

[f]Pub. L. No. 111-148, 124 Stat. 119 (2010), as amended by the Health Care and Education Reconciliation Act of 2010, Pub. L. No. 111-152, 124 Stat. 1029.

[g]Predictive analytics include the use of algorithms and models to analyze claims before payment is made in order to identify unusual or suspicious patterns or abnormalities in provider networks, claims billing patterns, and beneficiary utilization.

[h]Pub. L. No. 111-240, § 4241, 124 Stat. 2504, 2599.

CMS Has Strengthened Provider and Supplier Screening, but More Can Be Done to Improve Medicare Program Integrity

CMS has made progress in strengthening provider and supplier enrollment provisions, but needs to do more to identify and prevent potentially fraudulent providers and suppliers from participating in Medicare. Additional improvements to prepayment and postpayment claims review would help prevent and recover improper payments. Addressing payment vulnerabilities already identified could further help prevent or reduce fraud.

CMS Has Strengthened Certain Enrollment Screening Procedures since PPACA

PPACA authorized and CMS has implemented new provider and supplier enrollment procedures that address past weaknesses identified by GAO and HHS's Office of Inspector General (OIG) that allowed entities intent on committing fraud to enroll in Medicare. CMS has also implemented other measures intended to improve existing procedures. Specifically, to strengthen the existing screening activities conducted by CMS contractors, the agency added screenings of categories of provider and supplier enrollment applications by risk level, contracted with new national enrollment screening and site visit contractors, began imposing moratoria on new enrollment of certain types of providers and suppliers, and issued regulations requiring certain prescribers to enroll in Medicare.

Screening Provider and Supplier Enrollment Applications by Risk Level

CMS and OIG issued a final rule in February 2011 to implement many of the new screening procedures required by PPACA.[12] CMS designated three levels of risk—high, moderate, and limited—with different screening procedures for categories of Medicare providers and suppliers at each level. Providers and suppliers in the high-risk level are subject to the most rigorous screening.[13] (See table 2.) Based in part on our work and that of OIG, CMS designated newly enrolling home health agencies and

---

[12]*Medicare, Medicaid, and Children's Health Insurance Programs; Additional Screening Requirements, Application Fees, Temporary Enrollment Moratoria, Payment Suspensions and Compliance Plans for Providers and Suppliers*, 76 Fed. Reg. 5862 (Feb. 2, 2011). In discussing the final rule, CMS noted that Medicare had already employed a number of the screening practices described in PPACA to determine whether a provider is in compliance with federal and state requirements to enroll or to maintain enrollment in the Medicare program.

[13]PPACA specified that the enhanced screening procedures apply to new providers and suppliers beginning 1 year after the date of enactment (March 23, 2010) and to currently enrolled providers and suppliers 2 years after that date.

suppliers of durable medical equipment, prosthetics, orthotics, and supplies (DMEPOS) as high risk, and designated other providers and suppliers as lower risk levels. Providers and suppliers at all risk levels are screened to verify that they meet specific requirements established by Medicare, such as having current licenses or accreditation and valid Social Security numbers.[14] High- and moderate-risk providers and suppliers are also subject to unannounced site visits. Further, depending on the risks presented, PPACA authorizes CMS to require fingerprint-based criminal history checks. In March 2014, CMS awarded a contract that is to enable the agency to access Federal Bureau of Investigation information to help conduct those checks of high-risk providers and suppliers. PPACA also authorizes the posting of surety bonds for certain providers and suppliers.[15]

Table 2: Categories of Medicare Providers and Suppliers Designated by Risk Level for Enrollment Screening

Risk level	Categories of Medicare providers and suppliers
Limited	Physician or nonphysician practitioners and medical groups or clinics, with the exception of physical therapists and physical therapy groups. Ambulatory surgical centers, competitive acquisition programs/Part B vendors, end-stage renal disease facilities, federally qualified health centers, histocompatibility laboratories,[a] hospitals including critical access hospitals, Indian Health Service facilities, mammography screening centers, mass immunization roster billers,[b] organ procurement organizations, pharmacies newly enrolling or revalidating, radiation therapy centers, religious nonmedical health care institutions, rural health clinics, and skilled nursing facilities.
Moderate	Ambulance suppliers, community mental health centers, comprehensive outpatient rehabilitation facilities, hospice organizations, independent diagnostic testing facilities, independent clinical laboratories, physical therapy including physical therapy groups, portable X-ray suppliers, and currently enrolled (revalidating) home health agencies.
High	Prospective (newly enrolling) home health agencies and prospective (newly enrolling) suppliers of durable medical equipment, prosthetics, orthotics, and supplies.

Source: GAO analysis of CMS regulations. | GAO-14-712T

[a]The responsibility of the histocompatibility laboratory is to provide an evaluation of certain genetic data and pertinent patient immunologic risk factors that will allow the clinician and patient to decide which approaches to transplantation are in the patient's best interest.

[b]Mass immunization roster billers are providers and suppliers who enroll in the Medicare program to offer the influenza (flu) vaccinations to a large number of individuals, and they must be properly licensed in the states in which they plan to operate influenza clinics.

[14]Screening may include verification of the following: Social Security number; National Provider Identifier (NPI); National Practitioner Databank licensure; whether the provider has been excluded from federal health care programs by OIG; taxpayer identification number; and death of an individual practitioner, owner, authorized official, delegated official, or supervising physician.

[15]A surety bond is a three-party agreement in which a company, known as a surety, agrees to compensate the bondholder if the bond purchaser fails to keep a specified promise.

CMS has indicated that the agency will continue to review the criteria for its screening levels and will publish changes if the agency decides to update the assignment of screening levels for categories of Medicare providers and suppliers. Doing so could become important because the Department of Justice (DOJ) and HHS reported multiple convictions, judgments, settlements, or exclusions against types of providers and suppliers not currently at the high-risk level, including community mental health centers and ambulance suppliers.[16] CMS's implementation of accreditation for DMEPOS suppliers, and of a competitive bidding program, including in geographic areas thought to have high fraud rates, may be helping to reduce the risk of DMEPOS fraud.[17] While continued vigilance of DMEPOS suppliers is warranted, other types of providers may become more problematic in the future. Specifically, in September 2012 we reported that a range of providers have been the subjects of fraud investigations.[18] According to 2010 data from OIG and DOJ, over 10,000 providers and suppliers that serve Medicare, Medicaid, and Children's Health Insurance Program beneficiaries were involved in fraud investigations, including not only home health agencies and DMEPOS suppliers but also physicians, hospitals, and pharmacies.[19] In addition, the provider type constituting the largest percentage of subjects in criminal health care fraud investigations was medical facilities—including medical centers, clinics, or practices—which constituted almost a quarter of subjects in such investigations. DMEPOS suppliers made up a little over 16 percent of subjects.

---

[16]Department of Health and Human Services and the Department of Justice, *Health Care Fraud and Abuse Control Program Annual Report for Fiscal Year 2013* (Washington, D.C.: February 2014).

[17]Competitive bidding is a process in which suppliers of medical equipment and supplies compete for the right to provide their products on the basis of established criteria, such as quality and price. See GAO, *Medicare: Second Year Update for CMS's Durable Medical Equipment Competitive Bidding Program Round 1 Rebid*, GAO-14-156 (Washington, D.C.: Mar. 7, 2014).

[18]GAO, *Health Care Fraud: Types of Providers Involved in Medicare, Medicaid, and the Children's Health Insurance Program Cases*, GAO-12-820 (Washington, D.C.: Sept. 7, 2012).

[19]Medicaid is the federal-state program that covers acute health care, long-term care, and other services for certain low-income people. It is also one of the largest components of state budgets. Children's Health Insurance Program is the joint federal-state program that provides health coverage to children whose families have incomes that are low, but not low enough to qualify for Medicaid.

We are currently examining the ability of CMS's provider and supplier enrollment system to prevent and detect the continued enrollment of ineligible or potentially fraudulent providers and suppliers in Medicare. Specifically, we are assessing the process used to enroll and verify the eligibility of Medicare providers and suppliers in Medicare's Provider Enrollment, Chain, and Ownership System (PECOS) and the extent to which CMS's controls are designed to prevent and detect the continued enrollment of potentially ineligible or fraudulent providers and suppliers in PECOS. We plan to issue a report this winter.

Implementing National Enrollment Screening and Site Visit Contractors

CMS contracted with two new types of entities at the end of 2011 to assume centralized responsibility for two functions that had been the responsibility of multiple contractors. One of the new contractors is conducting automated screenings to check that existing and newly enrolling providers and suppliers have valid licensure, accreditation, and a National Provider Identifier (NPI), and are not on the OIG list of providers and suppliers excluded from participating in federal health care programs. The second contractor conducts site visits of providers and suppliers, except for DMEPOS suppliers, to determine whether sites are legitimate and the providers and suppliers meet certain Medicare standards.[20] A CMS official reported that, since the implementation of the PPACA screening requirements, the agency had revoked over 17,000 suspect providers' and suppliers' ability to bill the Medicare program.[21]

Establishing Moratoria on Enrollment of New Providers and Suppliers in Certain Areas

CMS has suspended enrollment of new home health providers and ground ambulance suppliers in certain fraud "hot spots" and other geographic areas. In July 2013, CMS first exercised its authority granted by PPACA to establish temporary moratoria on enrolling new home health agencies in Chicago and Miami, and new ambulance suppliers in Houston.[22] In January 2014, CMS extended its first moratoria and added

---

[20]Site visits for DMEPOS suppliers are to continue to be conducted by the contractor responsible for their enrollment. In addition, CMS at times exercises its authority to conduct a site visit or request its contractors to conduct a site visit for any Medicare provider or supplier.

[21]S. Agrawal, M.D., Deputy Administrator and Director, Center for Program Integrity, Centers for Medicare & Medicaid Services, *Preventing Medicare Fraud: How Can We Best Protect Seniors and Taxpayers?*, testimony before the Senate Special Aging Committee, 113th Cong., 2nd sess., March 26, 2014.

[22]Under the moratoria, existing providers and suppliers can continue to deliver and bill for services, but no new provider and supplier applications will be approved in these areas. CMS re-evaluates the need for such moratoria every 6 months.

enrollment moratoria for new home health agency providers in Fort Lauderdale, Detroit, Dallas, and Houston, and new ambulance suppliers in Philadelphia. These moratoria are scheduled to be in effect until July 2014, unless CMS extends or lifts them. CMS officials cited areas of potential fraud risk, such as a disproportionate number of providers and suppliers relative to beneficiaries and extremely high utilization as rationales for suspending new enrollments of home health providers or ground ambulance suppliers in these areas.

Requiring Certain Prescribers to Enroll in Medicare

CMS recently issued a final rule requiring prescribers of drugs covered within Medicare's prescription drug program, Part D, to enroll in Medicare by June 2015.[23] As a result of this rule, CMS is to screen these prescribers to verify that they meet specific requirements, such as having current licenses or accreditation and valid Social Security numbers. OIG has identified concerns with CMS oversight of fraud, waste, and abuse in Part D, including the contractors tasked with this work. A June 2013 OIG report found that the Part D program inappropriately paid for drugs ordered by individuals who clearly did not have the authority to prescribe, such as massage therapists, athletic trainers, home contractors, and interpreters.[24] OIG recommended, among other things, that there should be verification of prescribers' authority to prescribe drugs, and that CMS should ensure that Medicare does not pay for prescriptions from individuals without such authority. CMS agreed with OIG's recommendations and, in discussing the final rule, stated that this new enrollment requirement is to help ensure that Part D drugs are prescribed only by qualified physicians and eligible professionals. To continue to help address potential vulnerabilities in the Part D program, we are currently examining practices for promoting prescription drug program integrity and the extent to which CMS's oversight of Medicare Part D reflects those practices. We plan to issue a report this fall.

---

[23]*Medicare Program: Contract Year 2015 Policy and Technical Changes to the Medicare Advantage and the Medicare Prescription Drug Benefit Programs. 79 Fed. Reg. 29,844* (May 23, 2014).

[24]Department of Health and Human Services, Office of Inspector General, *Medicare Inappropriately Paid for Drugs Ordered by Individuals Without Prescribing Authority*, OEI-02-09-00608 (June 21, 2013).

Additional Enrollment Screening Could Help Ensure Potentially Fraudulent Providers and Suppliers Do Not Participate in Medicare

Although CMS has taken many needed actions, we and OIG have found that CMS has not fully implemented other enrollment screening actions authorized by PPACA.[25] These actions could help further reduce the enrollment of providers and suppliers intent on defrauding the Medicare program, which is important because identifying and prosecuting providers and suppliers engaged in potentially fraudulent activity is time consuming, resource intensive, and costly. These actions include issuing a rule to implement surety bonds for certain providers and suppliers, issuing a rule on provider and supplier disclosure requirements, and establishing the core elements for provider and supplier compliance programs.

Surety Bonds

PPACA authorized CMS to require a surety bond for certain types of at-risk providers and suppliers. Surety bonds may serve as a source for recoupment of erroneous payments. DMEPOS suppliers are currently required to post a surety bond at the time of enrollment.[26] CMS reported in April 2014 that it had not yet scheduled for publication a proposed rule to implement the PPACA surety bond requirement for other types of at-risk providers and suppliers—such as home health agencies and independent diagnostic testing facilities. In light of the moratoria that CMS has placed on enrollment of home health agencies in fraud "hot spots," implementation of this rule could help the agency address potential concerns for these at-risk providers across the Medicare program.

Providers and Suppliers Disclosure

CMS has not yet scheduled a proposed rule for publication for increased disclosures of prior actions taken against providers and suppliers enrolling or revalidating enrollment in Medicare, as authorized by PPACA, such as whether the provider or supplier has been subject to a payment

---

[25]GAO, *Medicare Program Integrity: CMS Continues Efforts to Strengthen the Screening of Providers and Suppliers,* GAO-12-351 (Washington, D.C.: Apr. 10, 2012).

[26]42 U.S.C. § 1395m(a)(16)(B). A DMEPOS surety bond is a bond issued by an entity guaranteeing that a DMEPOS supplier will fulfill its obligation to Medicare. If the obligation is not met, the surety bond is paid to Medicare. Medicare Program; Surety Bond Requirement for Suppliers of Durable Medical Equipment, Prosthetics, Orthotics, and Supplies (DMEPOS), 74 Fed. Reg. 166 (Jan. 2, 2009).

suspension from a federal health care program.[27] Agency officials had indicated that developing the additional disclosure requirements has been complicated by provider and supplier concerns about what types of information will be collected, what CMS will do with it, and how the privacy and security of this information will be maintained.

Compliance Program

CMS has not established the core elements of compliance programs for providers and suppliers, as required by PPACA. We previously reported that agency officials indicated that they had sought public comments on the core elements, which they were considering, and were also studying criteria found in OIG model plans for possible inclusion.[28] As of April 2014, CMS reported that it had not yet scheduled a proposed rule for publication.

Further Improvements to Prepayment and Postpayment Claims Review May Better Identify or Recover Improper Payments

Medicare uses prepayment review to deny claims that should not be paid and postpayment review to recover improperly paid claims. As claims go through Medicare's electronic claims payment systems, they are subjected to prepayment controls called "edits," most of which are fully automated; if a claim does not meet the criteria of the edit, it is automatically denied.[29] Other prepayment edits are manual; they flag a claim for individual review by trained staff who determine whether it should be paid. Due to the volume of claims, CMS has reported that less

---

[27]At the time of initial enrollment or revalidation of enrollment, PPACA requires providers and suppliers to disclose, in a form and manner and at such time as determined by the Secretary, any current or previous affiliation with another provider or supplier that has uncollected debt; has been or is subject to a payment suspension under a federal health care program; has been excluded from participation under Medicare, Medicaid, or State Children's Health Insurance Program; or has had its billing privileges denied or revoked. Pub. L. No. 111-148, § 6401(a), 124 Stat. 119, 750 (2010).

[28]A compliance program is an internal set of policies, processes, and procedures that a provider organization implements to help it act ethically and lawfully. In this context, a compliance program is intended to help provider and supplier organizations prevent and detect violations of Medicare laws and regulations. OIG has developed a series of voluntary compliance program guidance documents directed at various segments of the health care industry, such as hospitals, nursing homes, third-party billers, and durable medical equipment suppliers, to encourage the development and use of internal controls to monitor adherence to applicable statutes, regulations, and program requirements.

[29]Edits are instructions programmed in the systems to prevent payment of incomplete or incorrect claims. Some edits use provider enrollment information, while others use information on coverage or payment policies, to determine whether claims should be paid.

than 1 percent of Medicare claims are subject to manual medical record review by trained personnel.

Increased use of prepayment edits could help prevent improper Medicare payments. Our prior work found that, while use of prepayment edits saved Medicare at least $1.76 billion in fiscal year 2010, the savings could have been greater had prepayment edits been used more widely.[30] Based on an analysis of a limited number of national policies and local coverage determinations (LCD), we identified $14.7 million in payments in fiscal year 2010 that appeared to be inconsistent with four national policies and therefore improper.[31] We also found more than $100 million in payments that were inconsistent with three selected LCDs that could have been identified using automated edits. Thus, we concluded that more widespread implementation of effective automated edits developed by individual MACs in other MAC jurisdictions could also result in savings to Medicare. CMS has taken steps to improve the development of other types of prepayment edits that are implemented nationwide, as we recommended. For example, the agency has centralized the development and implementation of automated edits based on a type of national policy called national coverage determinations.[32] CMS has also modified its processes for identifying provider billing of services that are medically

---

[30]See GAO, *Medicare Program Integrity: Greater Prepayment Control Efforts Could Increase Savings and Better Ensure Proper Payment*, GAO-13-102 (Washington, D.C.: Nov. 13, 2012).

[31]Each Medicare administrative contractor (MAC) has the authority to develop LCDs that delineate the circumstances under which services are considered reasonable and necessary and are therefore covered in the geographic area where that MAC processes claims. These local policies cannot conflict with national coverage and payment policies established by CMS or by law. MACs' authority to develop LCDs leads to differences in Medicare coverage policy in different areas of the country. MACs may create prepayment edits either to implement their LCDs or to implement national Medicare policies set by CMS, although not every LCD or national policy is structured in a way that makes edit development feasible. CMS has responsibility for providing information and oversight to MACs with respect to their use of prepayment edits to promote effective stewardship of Medicare funds.

[32]CMS typically develops national coverage determinations for services that have the potential to affect a large number of beneficiaries and that have the greatest effect on the Medicare program. Development of national coverage determinations is a lengthy process, which requires review of clinical evidence and allows for public comment.

unlikely to prevent circumvention of automated edits designed to identify an unusually large quantity of services provided to the same patient.[33]

We also evaluated the implementation of CMS's Fraud Prevention System (FPS), which uses predictive analytic technologies as required by the Small Business Jobs Act of 2010 to analyze Medicare fee-for-service (FFS) claims on a prepayment basis. FPS identifies investigative leads for CMS's Zone Program Integrity Contractors (ZPIC), the contractors responsible for detecting and investigating potential fraud.[34] Implemented in July 2011, FPS is intended to help facilitate the agency's shift from focusing on recovering potentially fraudulent payments after they have been made, to detecting aberrant billing patterns as quickly as possible, with the goal of preventing these payments from being made. However, in October 2012, we found that, while FPS generated leads for investigators, it was not integrated with Medicare's payment-processing system to allow the prevention of payments until suspect claims can be determined to be valid. As of April 2014, CMS reported that while the FPS functionality to deny claims before payment had been integrated with the Medicare payment processing system in October 2013, the system did not have the ability to suspend payment until suspect claims could be investigated. In addition, while CMS directed the ZPICs to prioritize alerts generated by the system, in our work examining the sources of new ZPIC investigations in 2012, we found that FPS accounted for about 5 percent of ZPIC investigations in that year.[35] A CMS official reported in March 2014 that ZPICs are now using FPS as a primary source of leads for fraud investigations, though the official did not provide details on how much of ZPICs' work is initiated through the system.[36]

---

[33]CMS refers to these as Medically Unlikely Edits. These edits are designed to deny payment for services where the number of units billed exceeds the maximum number a provider would bill under most circumstances for a beneficiary on a single date of service.

[34]GAO, *Medicare Fraud Prevention: CMS Has Implemented a Predictive Analytics System, but Needs to Define Measures to Determine Its Effectiveness,* GAO-13-104 (Washington, D.C.: Oct. 15, 2012).

[35]GAO, *Medicare Program Integrity: Contractors Reported Generating Savings, but CMS Could Improve Its Oversight,* GAO-14-111 (Washington, D.C.: Oct. 25, 2013).

[36]S. Agrawal, *Preventing Medicare Fraud,* testimony before the Senate Special Aging Committee, March 26, 2014. Additionally, CMS has not published a report detailing the results of the second year of implementation of the FPS system, as required by the Small Business Jobs Act of 2010. The report was due in 2013.

Our prior work found that postpayment reviews are critical to identifying and recouping overpayments.[37] The use of national recovery audit contractors (RAC)[38] in the Medicare program is helping to identify underpayments and overpayments on a postpayment basis.[39] CMS began the program in March 2009 for Medicare FFS.[40] CMS reported that, as of the end of 2013, RACs collected $816 million for fiscal year 2014.[41] PPACA required the expansion of Medicare RACs to Parts C and D. CMS has implemented a RAC for Part D, and CMS said it plans to award a contract for a Part C RAC by the end of 2014. Moreover, in February 2014, CMS announced a "pause" in the RAC program as the agency makes changes to the program and starts a new procurement process for the next round of recovery audit contracts for Medicare FFS claims. CMS stated it anticipates awarding all five of these new Medicare FFS recovery audit contracts by the end of summer 2014.

Other contractors help CMS investigate potentially fraudulent FFS payments, but CMS could improve its oversight of their work. CMS contracts with ZPICs in specific geographic zones covering the nation. In October 2013, we found that the ZPICs reported that their actions, such as stopping payments on suspect claims, resulted in more than $250 million in savings to Medicare in calendar year 2012.[42] However, CMS lacks information on the timeliness of ZPICs' actions—such as the time it takes between identifying a suspect provider and taking actions to stop

[37]See GAO, *Medicare Fraud, Waste, and Abuse: Challenges and Strategies for Preventing Improper Payments*, GAO-10-844T (Washington, D.C.: June 15, 2010).

[38]These contractors are also referred to as Recovery Auditors.

[39]Recovery auditing has been used in various industries, including health care, to identify and collect overpayments for about 40 years.

[40]The Medicare Prescription Drug, Improvement, and Modernization Act of 2003 directed CMS to conduct a demonstration of the use of RACs in identifying underpayments and overpayments, and recouping overpayments in Medicare. Pub. L. No. 108-173, § 306, 117 Stat. 2066, 2256-57. Subsequently, the Tax Relief and Health Care Act of 2006 required CMS to implement a national RAC program by January 1, 2010. Pub. L. No. 109-432, div. B, title III, § 302, 120 Stat. 2922, 2991 (codified at 42 U.S.C. § 1395ddd(h)).

[41]See Centers for Medicare & Medicaid Services, *Medicare Fee for Service, National Recovery Audit Program, Quarterly Newsletter*, accessed Apr. 17, 2014, http://www.cms.gov/Research-Statistics-Data-and-Systems/Monitoring-Programs/Medicare-FFS-Compliance-Programs/Recovery-Audit-Program/Downloads/Medicare-FFS-Recovery-Audit-Program-1st-qtr-2014.pdf.

[42]GAO-14-111.

that provider from receiving potentially fraudulent Medicare payments—and would benefit from knowing whether ZPICs could save more money by acting more quickly. Thus we recommended that CMS collect and evaluate information on the timeliness of ZPICs' investigative and administrative actions. CMS did not provide comments on our recommendation. We are currently examining the activities of the CMS contractors, including ZPICs, that conduct postpayment claims reviews, and anticipate issuing a report later this summer. Our work is reviewing, among other things, whether CMS has a strategy for coordinating these contractors' postpayment claims review activities.

CMS has taken steps to improve use of two CMS information technology systems that could help analysts identify fraud after claims have been paid, but further action is needed. In 2011, we found that the Integrated Data Repository (IDR)—a central data store of Medicare and other data needed to help CMS program integrity staff and contractors detect improper payments of claims—did not include all the data that were planned to be incorporated by fiscal year 2010, because of technical obstacles and delays in funding.[43] As of March 2014, the agency had not addressed our recommendation, to develop reliable schedules to incorporate all types of IDR data, which could lead to additional delays in making available all of the data that are needed to support enhanced program integrity efforts and achieve the expected financial benefits. However, One Program Integrity (One PI)—a web-based portal intended to provide CMS staff and contractors with a single source of access to data contained in IDR, as well as tools for analyzing those data—is operational, and CMS has established plans and schedules for training all intended One PI users, as we also recommended in 2011. However, as of March 2014, CMS had not established deadlines for program integrity contractors to begin using One PI, as we recommended in 2011. Without these deadlines, program integrity contractors will not be required to use the system, and as a result, CMS may fall short in its efforts to ensure the widespread use and to measure the benefits of One PI for program integrity purposes.

---

[43]GAO, *Fraud Detection Systems: Centers for Medicare and Medicaid Services Needs to Ensure More Widespread Use*, GAO-11-475 (Washington, D.C.: June 30, 2011).

Addressing Identified Vulnerabilities Could Help Reduce Fraud

Having mechanisms in place to resolve vulnerabilities that could lead to improper payments, some of which are potentially fraudulent, is critical to effective program management, but our work has shown weaknesses in CMS's processes to address such vulnerabilities.[44] Both we and OIG have made recommendations to CMS to improve the tracking of vulnerabilities. In our March 2010 report on the RAC demonstration program, we found that CMS had not established an adequate process during the demonstration or in planning for the national program to ensure prompt resolution of vulnerabilities that could lead to improper payments in Medicare; further, the majority of the most significant vulnerabilities identified during the demonstration were not addressed.[45] In December 2011, OIG found that CMS had not resolved or taken significant action to resolve 48 of 62 vulnerabilities reported in 2009 by CMS contractors specifically charged with addressing fraud.[46] We and OIG recommended that CMS have written procedures and time frames to ensure that vulnerabilities were resolved. CMS has indicated that it is now tracking vulnerabilities identified from several types of contractors through a single vulnerability tracking process, and the agency has developed some written guidance on the process. In 2012, we examined that process and found that, while CMS informs Medicare administrative contractors (MAC) about vulnerabilities that could be addressed through prepayment edits, the agency does not systematically compile and disseminate information about effective local edits to address such vulnerabilities.[47] Specifically,

---

[44]Federal internal control standards state that an agency should have policies and procedures to ensure that (1) the findings of all audits and reviews are promptly evaluated, (2) decisions are made about the appropriate response to these findings, and (3) actions are taken to correct or resolve the issues promptly. These are all aspects of internal control, which is the component of an organization's management that provides reasonable assurance that the organization achieves effective and efficient operations, reliable financial reporting, and compliance with applicable laws and regulations. Internal control standards provide a framework for identifying and addressing major performance challenges and areas at greatest risk for mismanagement. See GAO, *Internal Control Standards: Internal Control Management and Evaluation Tool*, GAO-01-1008G (Washington, D.C.: August 2001).

[45]GAO, *Medicare Recovery Audit Contracting: Weaknesses Remain in Addressing Vulnerabilities to Improper Payments, Although Improvements Made to Contractor Oversight,* GAO-10-143 (Washington, D.C.: Mar. 31, 2010).

[46]Department of Health and Human Services, Office of Inspector General, *Addressing Vulnerabilities Reported by Medicare Benefit Integrity Contractors*, OEI-03-10-00500 (December 2011).

[47]GAO-13-102.

we recommended that CMS require MACs to share information about the underlying policies and savings related to their most effective edits, and CMS generally agreed to do so. In addition, in 2011 CMS began requiring MACs to report on how they had addressed certain vulnerabilities to improper payment, some of which could be addressed through edits.

We also made recommendations to CMS to address the millions of Medicare cards that display beneficiaries' Social Security numbers, which increases beneficiaries' vulnerability to identity theft.[48] In August 2012, we recommended that CMS (1) select an approach for removing Social Security numbers from Medicare cards that best protects beneficiaries from identity theft and minimizes burdens for providers, beneficiaries, and CMS; and (2) develop an accurate, well-documented cost estimate for such an option. In September 2013, we further recommended that CMS (1) initiate an information technology project for identifying, developing, and implementing changes for the removal of Social Security numbers; and (2) incorporate such a project into other information technology initiatives. HHS concurred with our recommendations and agreed that removing the numbers from Medicare cards is an appropriate step toward reducing the risk of identity theft. However, the department also stated that CMS could not proceed with changes without agreement from other agencies, such as the Social Security Administration, and that funding was also a consideration. Thus, CMS has not yet taken action to address these recommendations. We are currently examining other options for updating and securing Medicare cards, including the potential use of electronic-card technologies, and expect to issue a report early next year.

In conclusion, although CMS has taken some important steps to identify and prevent fraud through increased provider and supplier screening and other actions, the agency must continue to improve its efforts to reduce fraud, waste, and abuse in the Medicare program. Identifying the nature, extent, and underlying causes of improper payments, and developing adequate corrective action processes to address vulnerabilities, are essential prerequisites to reducing them. As CMS continues its implementation of PPACA and Small Business Jobs Act provisions,

---

[48]GAO, *Medicare Information Technology: Centers for Medicare and Medicaid Services Needs to Pursue a Solution for Removing Social Security Numbers from Cards,* GAO-13-761 (Washington, D.C.: Sept. 10, 2013) and GAO, *CMS Needs an Approach and a Reliable Cost Estimate for Removing Social Security Numbers from Medicare Cards,* GAO-12-831 (Washington, D.C.: Aug. 1, 2012).

GAO-14-712T

additional evaluation and oversight will help determine whether implementation of these provisions has been effective in reducing improper payments. We are investing resources in a body of work that assesses CMS's efforts to refine and improve its fraud detection and prevention abilities. Notably, we are currently assessing potential use of electronic-card technologies, which can help reduce Medicare fraud. We are also examining the extent to which CMS's information system can help prevent and detect the continued enrollment of ineligible or potentially fraudulent providers and suppliers in Medicare. Additionally, we have a study under way examining CMS's oversight of fraud, waste, and abuse in Medicare Part D to determine whether the agency has adopted certain practices for ensuring the integrity of that program. We are also examining CMS's oversight of some of the contractors that conduct reviews of claims after payment. These studies are focused on additional actions for CMS that could help the agency more systematically reduce potential fraud in the Medicare program.

Chairman Murphy, Ranking Member DeGette, and Members of the Subcommittee, this concludes my prepared remarks. I would be pleased to respond to any questions you may have at this time.

GAO Contact and Staff Acknowledgments

For further information about this statement, please contact Kathleen M. King at (202) 512-7114 or kingk@gao.gov. Contact points for our Offices of Congressional Relations and Public Affairs may be found on the last page of this statement. Karen Doran, Assistant Director; Eden Savino; and Jennifer Whitworth were key contributors to this statement.

GAO-14-712T

Appendix I: Abbreviations

CMS	Centers for Medicare & Medicaid Services
DMEPOS	durable medical equipment, prosthetics, orthotics, and supplies
DOJ	Department of Justice
FFS	fee-for-service
FPS	Fraud Prevention System
HHS	Department of Health and Human Services
IDR	Integrated Data Repository
LCD	local coverage determination
MAC	Medicare administrative contractor
NPI	National Provider Identifier
OIG	Office of Inspector General
One PI	One Program Integrity
PECOS	Provider Enrollment, Chain, and Ownership System
PPACA	Patient Protection and Affordable Care Act
RAC	recovery audit contractor
ZPIC	Zone Program Integrity Contractor

Related GAO Products

Medicare: Further Action Could Improve Improper Payment Prevention and Recoupment Efforts. GAO-14-619T. Washington, D.C.: May 20, 2014.

Medicare Fraud: Progress Made, but More Action Needed to Address Medicare Fraud, Waste, and Abuse, GAO-14-560T. Washington, D.C.: April 30, 2014.

Medicare: Second Year Update for CMS's Durable Medical Equipment Competitive Bidding Program Round 1 Rebid. GAO-14-156. Washington, D.C.: March 7, 2014.

Medicare Program Integrity: Contractors Reported Generating Savings, but CMS Could Improve Its Oversight. GAO-14-111. Washington, D.C.: October 25, 2013.

Health Care Fraud and Abuse Control Program: Indicators Provide Information on Program Accomplishments, but Assessing Program Effectiveness Is Difficult. GAO-13-746. Washington, D.C.: September 30, 2013.

Medicare Information Technology: Centers for Medicare and Medicaid Services Needs to Pursue a Solution for Removing Social Security Numbers from Cards. GAO-13-761. Washington, D.C.: September 10, 2013

Medicare Program Integrity: Few Payments in 2011 Exceeded Limits under One Kind of Prepayment Control, but Reassessing Limits Could Be Helpful. GAO-13-430. Washington, D.C.: May 9, 2013.

High-Risk Series: An Update. GAO-13-283. Washington, D.C.: February 14, 2013.

Medicare Program Integrity: Greater Prepayment Control Efforts Could Increase Savings and Better Ensure Proper Payment. GAO-13-102. Washington, D.C.: November 13, 2012.

Medicare Fraud Prevention: CMS Has Implemented a Predictive Analytics System, but Needs to Define Measures to Determine Its Effectiveness. GAO-13-104. Washington, D.C.: October 15, 2012.

Health Care Fraud: Types of Providers Involved in Medicare, Medicaid, and the Children's Health Insurance Program Cases. GAO-12-820. Washington, D.C.: September 7, 2012.

Medicare: CMS Needs an Approach and a Reliable Cost Estimate for Removing Social Security Numbers from Medicare Cards. GAO-12-831. Washington, D.C.: August 1, 2012.

Program Integrity: Further Action Needed to Address Vulnerabilities in Medicaid and Medicare Programs. GAO-12-803T. Washington, D.C.: June 7, 2012.

Medicare: Review of the First Year of CMS's Durable Medical Equipment Competitive Bidding Program's Round 1 Rebid. GAO-12-693. Washington, D.C.: May 9, 2012.

Medicare Program Integrity: CMS Continues Efforts to Strengthen the Screening of Providers and Suppliers. GAO-12-351. Washington, D.C.: April 10, 2012.

Medicare Part D: Instances of Questionable Access to Prescription Drugs. GAO-11-699. Washington, D.C.: September 6, 2011.

Medicare Integrity Program: CMS Used Increased Funding for New Activities but Could Improve Measurement of Program Effectiveness. GAO-11-592. Washington, D.C.: July 29, 2011.

Fraud Detection Systems: Centers for Medicare and Medicaid Services Needs to Ensure More Widespread Use. GAO-11-475. Washington, D.C.: June 30, 2011.

Medicare Fraud, Waste, and Abuse: Challenges and Strategies for Preventing Improper Payments. GAO-10-844T. Washington, D.C.: June 15, 2010.

Medicare Recovery Audit Contracting: Weaknesses Remain in Addressing Vulnerabilities to Improper Payments, Although Improvements Made to Contractor Oversight. GAO-10-143. Washington, D.C.: March 31, 2010.

Medicare: Thousands of Medicare Providers Abuse the Federal Tax System. GAO-08-618. Washington, D.C.: June 13, 2008.

Medicare: Improvements Needed to Address Improper Payments for Medical Equipment and Supplies. GAO-07-59. Washington, D.C.: January 31, 2007.

Medicare: More Effective Screening and Stronger Enrollment Standards Needed for Medical Equipment Suppliers. GAO-05-656. Washington, D.C.: September 22, 2005.

Medicare: CMS's Program Safeguards Did Not Deter Growth in Spending for Power Wheelchairs. GAO-05-43. Washington, D.C.: November 17, 2004.

9 781500 623685